ADVANC MICROSOFT EXCEL DATA ANALYTICS FOR BUSINESS

Author: John Slavio

TABLE OF CONTENTS

DISCLAIMER 4

ABOUT THE AUTHOR 5

INTRODUCTION TO ADVANCED EXCEL FUNCTIONS ... 6

OPTIMIZATION USING THE EXCEL SOLVER 13

SENSITIVITY ANALYSIS IN EXCEL 25

3-DIMENSIONAL FORMULA WITH HYPERLINKS.......... 39

DATA VALIDATION.. 45

DIFFERENT CHARTS AND THEIR APPLICATIONS 49

USING CORRELATIONS... 87

DATA FILTERS... 91

DATA CONSOLIDATION.. 96

OTHER FUNCTIONS... 101

CONCLUSION... 110

DISCLAIMER

ABOUT THE AUTHOR

John Slavio is a programmer who is passionate about the reach of the internet and the interaction of the internet with daily devices. He has automated several home devices to make them "smart" and connect them to high-speed internet. His passions involve computer security, iOT, hardware programming, and blogging.

INTRODUCTION TO ADVANCED EXCEL FUNCTIONS

What is the difference between Basic or Moderate Excel Users and Advanced Excel Users

There are a number of differences between the basic or moderate Excel user and advanced level Excel users. Excel is a massive program that has its own programming language and is very good for all sorts of applications from accounting, to marketing, to data science, and the list just goes on. Pretty much, if it includes numbers you can do something with it inside of Excel. The difference between the basic or moderate user and the advanced Excel user is that the advanced user is capable of exploiting the full potential of the Excel program.

Advanced Formulas

One of the quintessential steps to being an advanced user of Excel is learning the different Advanced formulas that Excel has. For instance, almost everyone utilizes the SUMIF at some point in their usage of extended Excel, but very rarely will they need to touch on SUMIFS. Unlike the original, this one takes as many if statements as you can possibly give it which makes it very versatile whenever you're trying to crunch down giant numbers. There are also array-formulas, formula auditing, and circular references. We will go over some of the more advanced formulas inside of this book.

Tables, Charts, and Formatting

Another one of the more advanced aspects of Excel is the level of ability that you have with the tables, formatting, and charting inside of the program. There are a massive number of tools available for these three different categories. There is a section specifically built around showing you how to use almost all of the charts that Excel has available to you. Even more mind-blowing is the fact that you can create charts within charts. Being able to use the various charts improves your ability to explain vast quantities of data. Not everyone will need to use this but if you are trying to explain a very key component of the industry you are working in and you have to track its location in the overall picture then you're going to need something like this. An example of this is if you look at your workspace and the different departments, and then you drill down into the sections within each department, and then the sub-section of those sections. In a regular graphing program, it's difficult to even just get a graph to be related to another graph, Excel can give you graphs within graphs within graphs.

Conditional Formatting

If you have ever tried to manually find the employee that seems to be the least productive member of the staff, or you have been trying to find the elements in a work station that seem to be causing the most problems, then you have obviously been missing out on conditional formatting. Conditional formatting allows you to set conditional rules that will highlight the specific type of element you are looking for so that even if you have line upon line upon line of data, you can still easily search for the item you're looking for. Conditional formatting is not very well known and is one of the more advanced features of Excel because it requires a lot of know-how on how to do it and there are not many resources in order to learn it.

Pivots

If you are going to look at a ton of data, you cannot do it without a pivot table or a pivot report. These two items are absolutely key for advanced users of Excel that are going to be looking at massive quantities of data simply because of how powerful they are as they allow you to do things like slicing, grouping, summarizing, and filtering of different metrics. Additionally, you can use pivoting to generate automatic tables and Excel actually does this whenever it recommends a table for you. Understanding how to use the pivot tool is absolutely vital whenever it comes to Advanced usage of Excel.

Excel Language and Macros

Macros and Excel programming are beyond the scope of this book but if you truly want to use the full power of Excel then learning Excel's language is vital. The most advanced users can actually figure out the routine that they have to follow on a daily basis and if they know how to program in the language of Excel then they can automate all of the steps it takes to do their job. There are individuals that work at companies that automate their work and are just there to make sure that the automation doesn't mess up or that whenever something happens because of the automation, they are able to step in and fix the issue. While it can go wrong because you are automating, it is a very powerful tool that will free up a lot of unproductive time.

Simulators and Solvers

If you are using any data science or medical science or anything that requires you to take an enormous amount of data and crunch them into something understandable, then learning how to use data tables, solvers, and even simulations will help you. The reason why each of these is important is that they serve a different aspect of how to convey the data that you have. For instance, a data table is usually to help quantify the problems that are practical in your industry and crunch the massive amount of data associated with those problems. A solver works as a solution finder by iterating through all the possibilities to see which ones will provide you with the most benefits. Lastly, you have simulations, and simulations provide you with a real-world view of the data that you're working with so that it is more in tune with a less predictable world. Due to the expansiveness of simulations, we will not be covering that in this book.

Excel Software Integration

Finally, the most advanced users of the Excel program are the users that integrate Excel into other programs. As a programmer, I know that I can utilize Excel inside of my program to both bring numbers into my program and then spit numbers out of my program so that they can be utilized by either Excel or another program. This is absolutely vital for use with programs like SolidWorks, that allow you to generate a statistical table of vector points for an object so that you can have a coordinate system of the size of your Object. To you, this may not seem important but to a person who works with 3D modeling, some model printers do not directly work with SolidWorks. So you need to be able to feed information into the model machine to print out the material that you wanted to print out and almost all model printers utilize Excel spreadsheets.

This is Not going to be Everything

Excel is a massive program and to show you everything would be to recreate the Excel manual in a more readable format. Instead, this book is going to highlight some of the more advanced capabilities of Excel that can be used by almost everyone. I'll discuss most of the equations and formulas that we have mentioned so far, as well as others that you can apply when using Excel. There is much more than what is provided within this book but we will go over a lot of Excel formulas and methodologies that help more advanced users get a secure footing in a very complex environment.

OPTIMIZATION USING THE EXCEL SOLVER – HOW TO WITH POSSIBLE APPLICATIONS

I know that we've just met, but I need to ask a favor of you. I'll give you around 2 minutes to complete this favor and all I want you to do is look at the image below and tell me, which application will provide me the greatest profit after calculating for all of the variables.

Developer	App Cost by Hour	App Revenue	Units Sold	Maintence Time/hr	Constraints	
Lotlux	$ 5.45	$ 30.18	55	6.72	Hours in a Business Month	480
Aerified	$ 28.05	$ 2.73	89	6.88	Max Labor Hours	160
Zathin	$ 10.31	$ 24.70	37	3.09	Maintenance cost	510
Bytecard	$ 33.18	$ 40.91	86	2.70		
Tresom	$ 15.73	$ 14.80	8	7.41		
Prodder	$ 44.20	$ 43.24	41	9.90		
Duobam	$ 28.90	$ 7.60	54	5.31		
Cookley	$ 11.64	$ 33.91	23	8.09		
Y-find	$ 34.70	$ 25.69	23	0.07		
Fixflex	$ 26.93	$ 21.51	18	9.74		

Profit		Maintenance Cost	Total Profit	Total Units Sold
Lotlux	$ 1,659.90	$ 36.62	$ 8,977.11	434
Aerified	$ 242.97	$ 192.98		
Zathin	$ 913.90	$ 31.86		
Bytecard	$ 3,518.26	$ 89.59		
Tresom	$ 118.40	$ 116.56		
Prodder	$ 1,772.84	$ 437.58		
Duobam	$ 410.40	$ 153.46		
Cookley	$ 779.93	$ 94.17		
Y-find	$ 590.87	$ 2.43		
Fixflex	$ 387.18	$ 262.30		

Alright, pencils down, let's see the results. Oh … wait, most of you have not finished. Honestly, if you couldn't do it in under 2 minutes, that's okay because I don't think anyone can do that amount of complicated math in that time. However, if you knew how to use a Solver, you could.

Learning How to Use the Excel Solver

You will find that the solver is not in your application by default and you will need to go into your Add-ins and turn it on. Additionally, there are a few things that you need to keep track of… actually, no there's not. You see, the solver doesn't presume to know what you want to solve and, so it is left open as much as possible. This also means that you can generally use a Solver with practically everything. However, for this example we are going to keep it rather simple. We have a list of 10 different developers that our fictitious company owns and operates and each of those developers charge a different price and sell units at different paces. We will need to figure out which application seems to be making us the most amount of money. This is the difficult part and the part that we want to use our solver for. Now the important part to note is that we've already set up some constraints in our Excel sheet and that is that there are only so many hours in the month, there is a maximum number of hours that we can dedicate to labor, and that there is a cap on the maintenance costs. Our goal here is simply to see which app will give us the most bang for our buck so that we know which application to set up our marketing around. Therefore, I am going to go with the basic route of trying to lower maintenance costs as this would significantly maximize the profit. I know how I would do this, but we need to know how to do it in solver because we're going to build on that. We click on Solver and this pops up

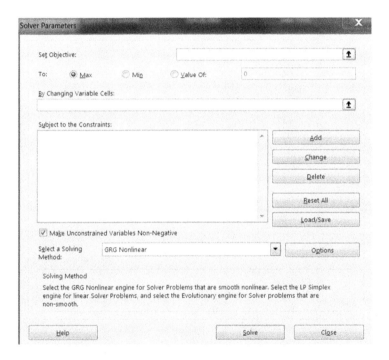

This is definitely going to be complicated, right? Actually, no. The Objective is what you want to maximize and since we want to maximize our profits, I need to select the cell that represents the profit.

That sets my objective, but we have the option to maximize, minimize, or set a specific target number. We could say that we want max because we set our objective to maximize profits, but if we were looking to minimize labor then our overall labor count would be the Set Objective and we would have selected different variables. Now we need to let it have the variables that it is going to change to *get* those maximized profits. In our naive example, we're going to choose the hours worked on maintenance. Finally, we'll click on Add and select the cell for Max Labor Hours and set the values in Maintenance time to be less than that. We click okay and now we have something like this:

Now when we click on solve, we will almost immediately see why this is naive.

App Revenue	Units Sold	Maintence Time/hr	Constraints	
$ 30.18	55	0.00	Hours in a Business Month	480
$ 2.73	89	0.00	Max Labor Hours	160
$ 24.70	37	0.00	Maintenance cost	$10
$ 40.91	86	0.00		
$ 14.80	8	0.00		
$ 43.24	41	0.00		
$ 7.60	54	0.00		
$ 33.91	23	0.00		
$ 25.69	23	0.00		
$ 21.51	18	0.00		

Maintenance Cost		Total Profit	Total Units Sold	
$ -		$ 10,394.65	434	
$ -				
$ -				
$ -				
$ -				
$ -				
$ -				
$ -				
$ -				
$ -				

Technically, Solver did exactly what we wanted but the problem is that our data is not constrained enough. We do not have calculations set to account for what happens if all the maintenance time is unaccounted for. Luckily, we are given the option to restore our previous values, which we will do.

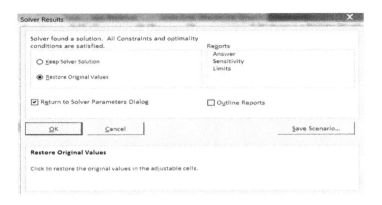

As of right now, most of this Excel sheet is programmed in an extremely basic manner with the maintenance time not actually having a positive effect on the profit. This is because the Profit margin, where the Total Profit is calculated from, does not factor in the maintenance time that should be a set variable. Therefore, let's move over to something that will work and that is to base this on the Units Sold.

For this constraint, we are going to say that we want to produce the exact same number of units but we still want to maximize profits. Even though we cannot target maintenance time, we can still target the profit by figuring out which apps sell the best. How do I know that it will do this? Well, by running Trace Precedents in the Formula Auditing section.

19

App Cost by Hour	App Revenue	Units Sold	Maintence Time/hr	Co
$ 5.45	$ 30.18	55	6.72	Hot
$ 28.05	$ 2.73	89	6.88	Ma:
$ 10.31	$ 24.70	37	3.09	Mai
$ 33.18	$ 40.91	86	2.70	
$ 15.73	$ 14.80	8	7.41	
$ 44.20	$ 43.24	41	9.90	
$ 28.90	$ 7.60	54	5.31	
$ 11.64	$ 33.91	23	8.09	
$ 34.70	$ 25.69	23	0.07	
$ 26.93	$ 21.51	18	9.74	

Profit	Maintenance Cost	Total Profit	Tot.
$ 1,659.90	$ 36.62	$ 8,977.11	
$ 242.97	$ 192.98		

What this tells me is that the profit of an app is determined by the App Revenue multiplied by the Units Sold.

Profit	Maintenance Cost	Total Profit
$ 1,659.90	$ 36.62	$ 8,977.11
$ 242.97	$ 192.98	

By following the dotted line of running Trace Precedents on just the Total profit, we can see that this takes into account the maintenance cost and the profit. Therefore, by basing this on the units sold, we will be able to change the app revenue and since the maintenance time will never change, it allows us to see which app sells the best.

So, first, we reopen Solver and click the Reset All option to get everything back to normal. We then reselect the Total Profit as our Set

Objective with a goal of maximizing it, select the column of Units Sold

for the variables that they will be able to change, and, finally, we make

sure that the units will amount to the same quantity by setting it to Total

Unit Sold. Finally, we click on Solve.

Developer	App Cost by Hour	App Revenue	Units Sold	Maintence Time/hr	Constraints	
Lotlux	$ 5.45	$ 30.18	434	6.72	Hours in a Business Month	480
Aerified	$ 28.05	$ 2.73	434	6.88	Max Labor Hours	160
Zathin	$ 10.31	$ 24.70	434	3.09	Maintenance cost	$10
Bytecard	$ 33.18	$ 40.91	434	2.70		
Tresom	$ 15.73	$ 14.80	434	7.41		
Prodder	$ 44.20	$ 43.24	434	9.90		
Duobam	$ 28.90	$ 7.60	434	5.31		
Cookley	$ 11.64	$ 33.91	434	8.09		
Y-find	$ 34.70	$ 25.69	434	0.07		
Fixflex	$ 26.93	$ 21.51	434	9.74		

	Profit	Maintenance Cost	Total Profit	Total Units Sold
Lotlux	$ 13,098.12	$ 36.62	$ 105,029.64	434
Aerified	$ 1,184.82	$ 192.98		
Zathin	$ 10,719.80	$ 31.86		
Bytecard	$ 17,754.94	$ 89.59		
Tresom	$ 6,423.20	$ 116.56		
Prodder	$ 18,766.16	$ 437.58		
Duobam	$ 3,298.40	$ 153.46		
Cookley	$ 14,716.94	$ 94.17		
Y-find	$ 11,149.46	$ 2.43		
Fixflex	$ 9,335.34	$ 262.30		

As we see here, the units sold is maximized to 434, which is a

bad answer. At this point, this has become slightly annoying *and*

hilarious at the same time. Sure, we maximized profit but, once again,

our process has a problem with it. What the Solver understood was that

so long as each cell was equal to 434, we would achieve our result. This

is actually because the Total Units Sold was hard coded *and* we looked

at the constraint wrong. You see, if we set the Total Units Sold to be the *calculated* SUM of all the Units Sold, as in use the function to do this, it will change if the variables change. This means that we can have the Solver focus on keeping the Total Units Sold to a specific 434 and when it changes the variables, it will make sure that their SUM does not exceed that amount. Therefore, the new Solver looks like this:

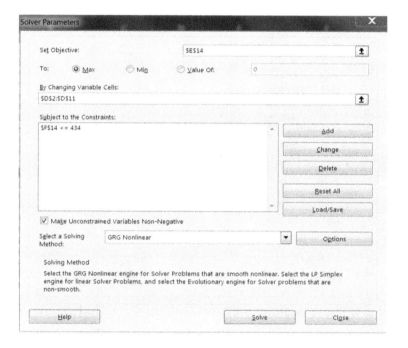

And when we click on Solve, we actually get our solution!

Developer	App Cost by Hour		App Revenue		Units Sold	Maintence Time/hr	Constraints	
Lotlux	$	5.45	$	30.18	0	6.72	Hours in a Business Month	480
Aerified	$	28.05	$	2.73	0	6.88	Max Labor Hours	160
Zathin	$	10.31	$	24.70	0	3.09	Maintenance cost	$10
Bytecard	$	33.18	$	40.91	0	2.70		
Tresom	$	15.73	$	14.80	0	7.41		
Prodder	$	44.20	$	43.24	434	9.90		
Duobam	$	28.90	$	7.60	0	5.31		
Cookley	$	11.64	$	33.91	0	8.09		
Y-find	$	34.70	$	25.69	0	0.07		
Fixflex	$	26.93	$	21.51	0	9.74		

	Profit		Maintenance Cost		Total Profit		Total Units Sold	
Lotlux	$	-	$	36.62	$	17,348.62	434.0000031	
Aerified	$	-	$	192.98				
Zathin	$	-	$	31.86				
Bytecard	$	-	$	89.59				
Tresom	$	-	$	116.56				
Prodder	$	18,766.16	$	437.58				
Duobam	$	-	$	153.46				
Cookley	$	-	$	94.17				
Y-find	$	-	$	2.43				
Fixflex	$	-	$	262.30				

So, it turns out that even though our Prodder has the highest amount of time for maintenance and the highest App Cost per hour of Maintenance, it is our highest selling application!

Possible Applications

As complex as the solver may seem, it actually shows you just how robust it can truly be whenever figuring out massive quantities of data. I'm not sure that I could have created a formula within an hour to actually calculate which one would sell the most and I would need to go through each of the units in the units sold section and Max it out to simply see which one sold the best. This is what the solver ultimately did. However, if you are looking at performance charts and you want to focus on a specific trait or if you are looking at 1000 different checking accounts, the solver is very useful. The solver is built to solve massively complex problems, but it can also solve some really simple ones if you don't want to spend the time to build the formulas needed to solve them yourself. So long as you understand how to place the constraints, the solver can be a very powerful tool in every industry that has anything to do with numbers.

SENSITIVITY ANALYSIS IN EXCEL – HOW TO WITH APPLICATIONS

What is Sensitivity Analysis?

Sensitivity analysis is a little bit different than many of the items that you work with inside of Excel because sensitivity analysis is actually a way of predicting where a specific goal is going to be based on changes in the variables that those goals rely on. A good example of this is the total product sold and the total profit from the examples that we've been going through. When we learned how to use the Excel solver, we also learned the same exact process as the sensitivity analysis otherwise known as the "What if analysis" found in the forecast section of the data menu. In our Excel solver section, we wanted to find the product that would give us the most amount of money based on the total Units Sold and we put a cap on the number of units that were sold. Essentially, we asked "what if we focused on one product rather than any other product? Which product would be the best product?" and this represents your basic what-if analysis. Our target goal is the total profit and our changing variable is just how many units of each item is being sold. This comprises the basic necessities that make up a sensitivity analysis.

How to do a sensitivity analysis in Excel

As I have already discussed, a Sensitivity Analysis is really just seeing what happens to a final variable when you change its dependents, which means there are several ways to do this. First, let's go over the very overly simplistic way that we do this manually. Again, we are going to use this data:

	A	B	C	D	E	F	G
1	Developer	App Cost by Hour	App Revenue	Units Sold	Maintence Time/hr	Constraints	
2	Lotlux	$ 5.45	$ 30.18	55	6.72	Hours in a Business Month	480
3	Aerified	$ 28.05	$ 2.73	89	6.88	Max Labor Hours	160
4	Zathin	$ 10.31	$ 24.70	37	3.09	Maintenance cost	$10
5	Bytecard	$ 33.18	$ 40.91	86	2.70		
6	Tresom	$ 15.73	$ 14.80	8	7.41		
7	Prodder	$ 44.20	$ 43.24	41	9.90		
8	Duobam	$ 28.90	$ 7.60	54	5.31		
9	Cookley	$ 11.64	$ 33.91	23	8.09		
10	Y-find	$ 34.70	$ 25.69	23	0.07		
11	Fixflex	$ 26.93	$ 21.51	18	9.74		
12							
13		Profit	Maintenance Cost		Total Profit	Total Units Sold	
14	Lotlux	$ 1,659.90	$ 36.62		$ 8,977.11		434
15	Aerified	$ 242.97	$ 192.98				
16	Zathin	$ 913.90	$ 31.86				
17	Bytecard	$ 3,518.26	$ 89.59				
18	Tresom	$ 118.40	$ 116.56				
19	Prodder	$ 1,772.84	$ 437.58				
20	Duobam	$ 410.40	$ 153.46				
21	Cookley	$ 779.93	$ 94.17				
22	Y-find	$ 590.87	$ 2.43				
23	Fixflex	$ 387.18	$ 262.30				

Now, at this point, we have already made Total Profit dependent on the Units Sold variable by making the Profit variables dependent on

26

the App Revenue multiplied by the Units Sold. This means to do a manual Sensitivity Analysis, we just have to change one of the Units Sold. For instance, what if we didn't sell any Lotlux applications? Well, it is quite obvious that we would entirely lose the profit margin for that application. This is how we would do this manually. However, what if wanted to run this automatically to see how this would change the entire spreadsheet? We would want to run a Scenario, which is the very first option in the What-If Analysis and it brings up this dialogue box:

Scenario Manager

Scenarios:

No Scenarios defined. Choose Add to add scenarios.

Add...
Delete
Edit...
Merge...
Summary...

Changing cells:
Comment:

Show   Close

We are going to run this same calculation via a Scenario, which will seem useless for now, but it has a purpose. To add a scenario, like the one we just went over, you click on the Add button. This brings up the first of two dialogue boxes:

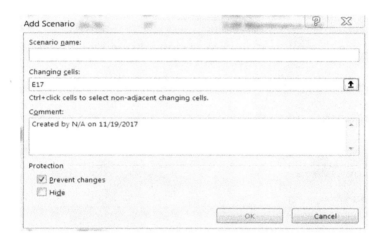

This is going to ask for a name for the scenario, the cell that is going to affect the change, and then some information to remind you or let someone else know why that scenario was created. We'll call this one Lotlux failure and set the Changing Cells to the Units Sold. It will now bring up the next menu, which is the Scenario values dialogue box (part 2) and this is where you provide the criteria or the condition that you want to see happen that will affect the remainder of the variables. We are just going to set this to 0.

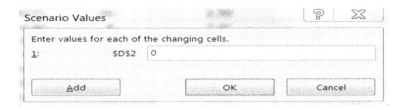

Now, we could hit the Show button when it goes back to the Scenario Manager, but I'm going to showcase how this scenario could be beneficial. Now, almost every Sales Manager loves Black Friday because it usually means that their profit margins skyrocket, but this is also at a loss to the Revenue per Product. This means we need two more Scenarios: one where all the Units Sold triple but also one where the App Revenue stays the same or is significantly reduced. Let's say that the rest of the products saw a benefit because we lowered their prices but not Lotlux. Therefore, we will add two more Scenarios called Black Friday Profit and Black Friday Units.

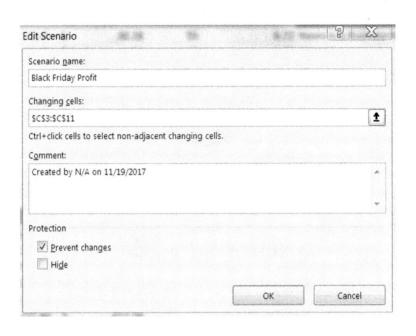

Now we have all the scenarios that we want:

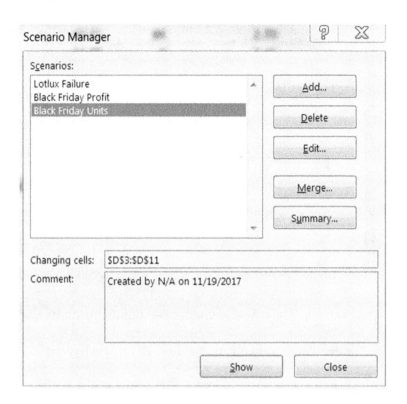

Now that I have all of the scenarios set, I can choose what I want to see but let's go ahead and apply everything to see exactly what would happen in this basic example.

	A	B	C	D	E	F	G
1	Developer	App Cost by Hour	App Revenue	Units Sold	Maintence Time/hr	Constraints	
2	Lotlux	$ 5.45	$ 30.18	0	6.72	Hours in a Business Month	480
3	Aerified	$ 28.05	$ 1.37	178	6.88	Max Labor Hours	160
4	Zathin	$ 10.31	$ 12.35	74	3.09	Maintenance cost	$10
5	Bytecard	$ 33.18	$ 20.46	172	2.70		
6	Tresom	$ 15.73	$ 7.40	16	7.41		
7	Prodder	$ 44.20	$ 21.62	82	9.90		
8	Duobam	$ 28.90	$ 3.80	108	5.31		
9	Cookley	$ 11.64	$ 16.96	46	8.09		
10	Y-find	$ 34.70	$ 12.85	46	0.07		
11	Fixflex	$ 26.93	$ 10.76	36	9.74		
12							
13		Profit	Maintenance Cost		Total Profit	Total Units Sold	
14	Lotlux	$ -	$ 36.62		$ 7,317.21	758	
15	Aerified	$ 242.97	$ 192.98				
16	Zathin	$ 913.90	$ 31.86				
17	Bytecard	$ 3,518.26	$ 89.59				
18	Tresom	$ 118.40	$ 116.56				
19	Prodder	$ 1,772.84	$ 437.58				
20	Duobam	$ 410.40	$ 153.46				
21	Cookley	$ 779.93	$ 94.17				
22	Y-find	$ 590.87	$ 2.43				
23	Fixflex	$ 387.18	$ 262.30				
24							

As you see, while we did change the number of units sold and the price for each app, only our first rule really made any difference. This is because we didn't use randomized numbers and we just canceled out the two scenarios by division and product. In a real-world example, we would use the multiplicative of how many more items we sold given a price change on that day. This would significantly impact the spreadsheet. So, why would this be useful? First of all, it saves all the scenarios so that you don't have to go back and type in the equations manually every time you want to see a common scenario. Second, it is extremely easy to set up and keep track of multiple scenarios that you can then apply to see what each one will do. Lastly, since we know that our scenarios were applied three times, we can now hit the undo button 3 times to get back to our original values. To do this manually, you would need to save it as another file before you made all of those changes or save the original values in a separate file so that you could easily go back to them once you made the changes. For most of us, this can get quite confusing if you're trying to both see a cumulative change and singular changes.

Now, there are two more features inside of the What If section: Goal Seek and Data Table. The reason why I showed you the Scenario Manager is due to the simplicity of these additional two options. When you open up Goal Seek, you will see a dialogue box like this:

Goal Seek		?	X
Set cell:	C10		↑
To value:			
By changing cell:			↑
	OK		Cancel

The first option "Set cell" is the cell that you want to set your goal at so this cell, for our example, should be the number underneath Total Profit. Then the "To value" option is there for us to determine exactly what value we want to get to. Finally, the "By changing cell" is the variable that the program gets to change until it changes the current value to the "To value" variable. Basically, it is similar to what scenario does, but just for one input and one output.

The Data Table is a little different by comparison. It essentially does the same task but instead of solving for a singular cell, we solve for multiple cells. If you have ever needed to make a chart that says that you wanted to see how much money you would make on one item and compare that to the money you would make on another item if you sold the items at the same price but in different quantities, then this next example will show you a way to remove the tediousness of that task. When you click on Data Table, you will get a menu like this:

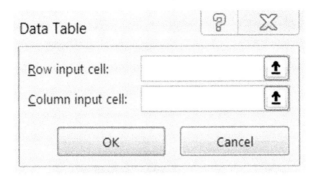

This can be pretty confusing at first if you have only ever dealt with Goal Seek and Scenario. Remember, Scenario is an expansion and a combination of Goal Seek and Data Table. In this case, we will use this as an example:

As you can see, we have Units Sold across the top and App Revenue down the left side. Units Sold is our Row Input while App Revenue is our Column Input. Now, if you notice, I left a blank space where the horizontal headers and column headers converge. This is where I am going to put in the calculation I want to use for my table, which is this:

=PRODUCT(A27,B26)

Now, I highlight that corner and drag it all the way over like

this:

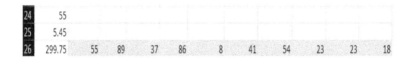

26	299.75	55	89	37	86	8	41	54	23	23	18
27	5.45										
28	28.05										
29	10.31										
30	33.18										
31	15.73										
32	44.2										
33	28.9										
34	11.64										
35	34.7										
36	26.93										

However, if I were to click on 55 and 5.45 as my values, I

would get a reference variable error. This is why I need to copy and

paste these numbers outside of the affected area. I also need to change

the equation so that it references variables outside of the selected area,

so the new formula will now become =PRODUCT(A:24,A:25). It

should now look like this:

24	55										
25	5.45										
26	299.75	55	89	37	86	8	41	54	23	23	18

Now we get down to the Row and Column variables. These are

actually interchangeable for the most part, for instance, I could put 55 in

36

the green category and 5.45 in the yellow category and because of my

equation, I would get the same result but the importance is in the

formatting. When the Data Table asks for a Row Input, it is asking for

the first variable it should start that will ultimately be iterated over via a

row format. Therefore, if I put 55 in A:27 it would need to be selected

as the Column input cell as it will be iterated over in a column format

but if I have it in the yellow like I do now, it needs to be in the Row

input cell. Therefore, what it finally looks like is this:

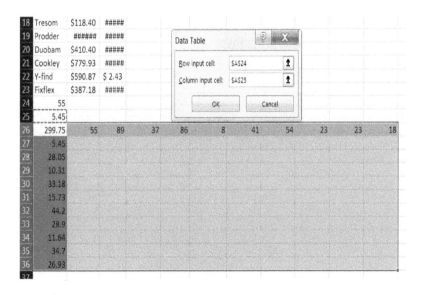

When we hit Okay, this happens:

26	299.75	55	89	37	86	8	41	54	23	23	18
27	5.45	299.75	485.05	201.65	468.7	43.6	223.45	294.3	125.35	125.35	98.1
28	28.05	1542.75	2496.5	1037.85	2412.3	224.4	1150.05	1514.7	645.15	645.15	504.9
29	10.31	567.05	917.59	381.47	886.66	82.48	422.71	556.74	237.13	237.13	185.58
30	33.18	1824.9	2953	1227.66	2853.5	265.44	1360.38	1791.72	763.14	763.14	597.24
31	15.73	865.15	1400	582.01	1352.8	125.84	644.93	849.42	361.79	361.79	283.14
32	44.2	2431	3933.8	1635.4	3801.2	353.6	1812.2	2386.8	1016.6	1016.6	795.6
33	28.9	1589.5	2572.1	1069.3	2485.4	231.2	1184.9	1560.6	664.7	664.7	520.2
34	11.64	640.2	1036	430.68	1001	93.12	477.24	628.56	267.72	267.72	209.52
35	34.7	1908.5	3088.3	1283.9	2984.2	277.6	1422.7	1873.8	798.1	798.1	624.6
36	26.93	1481.15	2396.8	996.41	2316	215.44	1104.13	1454.22	619.39	619.39	484.74

It has now taken the equation located where the column and row meet and it has applied it to each cell, such as the cell where 55 and 10.31 meet now becomes =PRODUCT(B26,A29) and this makes making a crossing data table a lot faster.

3-DIMENSIONAL FORMULA WITH HYPERLINKS

What is a 3-D Formula?

You actually use 3D formulas all the time but the problem is that many people simply can't conceptualize where that third dimension is coming from or even how the formulas have dimensions in the first place. Let's go over what the 2D formula is. Your 2D formula is simply your rows and your columns. For instance, if you wanted to take A26 and multiply that by C27 then you would have a formula of multiplication on a row and a column. This is what they mean by 2D because you are only ever working with two different dimensions inside of your sheet. Notice that I said that this was inside of your sheet because your sheet is the third dimension. Let's go over an example of a 3D formula just using sheets before we cover hyperlinks. Now, all I'm going to do is copy the sheet over and duplicate it for this example. To do that, you just hold down the Ctrl key and drag it over to the position that you want the spreadsheet at and then let go of your left click. Now

my data looks like this:

However, back in mock data 3 I am going to create a new

variable. This variable will be called quarterly profits and what it's

going to do is it's going to add up all of the quarterly profits represented

by the two different sheets that I created. In fact, in the spirit of calling

it quarterly profits, I am going to duplicate two more sheets just so that

it is an actual an addition of quarters. Now the formula that we utilize to

add up everything in a column and a row is usually the sum function so

I'm going to start with the sum function and then we'll get to the three-

dimensional part. Now that I have my sum function, I will begin to

select my data. The first thing that I want to click on is the cell where

the data is in this sheet, it's important to know where the data is because

in order to add the other cells in the other sheets, it has to be in this

exact spot otherwise you will have to click on the corresponding cell in each sheet or know beforehand what the cell reference is for each sheet. So, before I select my sheets, my sum function will look like this:

38	Quarterly Profits
39	=SUM(E14
40	

In order to select my sheets, I need to hold down shift and left click over each of the sheets that I want to do this with. My equation will now look like this:

=SUM('MOCK_DATA (3):MOCK_DATA (5)'!E14)

What this is doing is that it is looking through sheets MOCK_DATA(3) to the last item I clicked and then, inside of those sheets, it is finding the E14 cell for each one of them. If you wanted to do this yourself, you use this formula

'exact sheet name in single quotes'!cell

The "!" tells Excel that it is working with a third type of variable and so it assumes that whatever is in the single quotes is going to be a sheet name. I am quite certain you are seeing the ramifications of this. Well, here's the thing, it's great that we can do this but Microsoft wanted to see how far they could take this so they decided to make hyperlinking a possibility.

Hyperlinking Function

Now just to make sure that you know how to hyperlink we're going to cover the hyperlink functionality and it's pretty simple because all you need is the link that you want to hypertext to and the text you want to display for that hyperlink. The problem is that the function takes in cell items and not direct links or names unless you use double quotes. Therefore, if you want something to look nice you have to place a show name and an address in separate cells and then link to them. Ultimately, it will look like this:

f_x	=HYPERLINK(D39,E39)	
C	D	E
Google	www.google.com	Google

3D Hyperlinking Function

Now that you know what 3D formulas look like and how hyperlink is manually handled, we will now cover 3D hyperlinking, which is just as easy as the previous two. Unlike the previous two when you had full control over this, you will not always have full control over 3D hyperlinking inside of your spreadsheet. For this, all you need to do is right-click on a spreadsheet cell after you have given it a name. Then you click on the hyperlink option that will be at the bottom of the context menu that opens up. The key to this is the "link to" reference on the left-hand side because you start out with the ability to link in files and web pages but what we want is the "place in this document section". There, you will find a list of spreadsheets that you currently have open in that workbook and it will ask you for a cell reference so that whenever it jumps to the next spreadsheet it will land at that specific cell reference and then you will need to click on the appropriate spreadsheet name underneath the cell reference. This is how you link a cell to another spreadsheet in your workbook so that whenever you click on it, it will jump to that worksheet.

The Difference between a 3D Reference and a 3D Formula

Now, something you need to understand is the difference between a 3D reference and a 3D formula. Up until now, we have mostly been using a 3D reference such as using a cell to link to another spreadsheet cell. A 3D formula is a formula designed to use a variable found in another spreadsheet. Therefore, when you use the hyperlinking function to set a cell to relocate you towards another cell in another spreadsheet, you are using a 3D formula with hyperlinking. You can make this even more complex, but this is the most basic example of this Advanced technique.

DATA VALIDATION

What is Data Validation?

This answer seems very simple at first until you really think about it because the obvious answer is that data validation is a way for testing whether a variable or data point is something that you want or something you don't want. This makes a lot of sense, but it also is lacking in the representation of just how complex data validation can be if you try to manually validate for every single type of data point that exists. Well, in Excel, we have simplified this and boiled it down into a very simplistic way of understanding it. First, you select a column or row that you want to validate and then that entire column or row will be subject to a specific parameter. This is different from manually checking to see if every variable is the variable that matches what you need in order to get the data you want. Second, you do have to provide a condition and data validation.

Data Validation in Excel

Just like almost everything that we have worked with for the past couple of chapters, you will find the data validation button within the data tab but this time we are working with the data tools. It will look like this in the application:

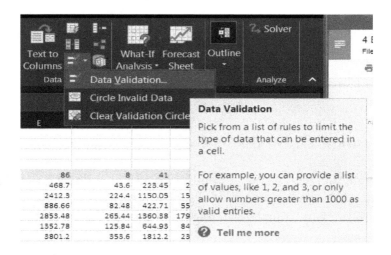

Make sure that you select a column or row before beginning the data validation process. After you have selected a column or row, click on the data validation icon, which will bring up the data validation dialog box. By default, the data validation dialog box is set to allow any type of variable to exist within a cell and this is the permission that we want to change inside of Excel. Let's say that I choose the row of numbers found in the table that we were working with earlier. Just for this example, we're going to make sure that the value cannot go above 30,000 or below 20.

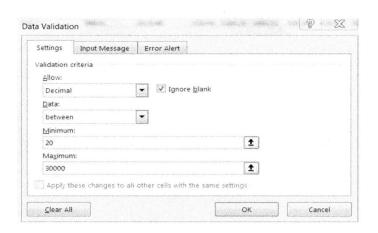

However, I also want to make sure the user knows why they are getting the error and sometimes we want to also let them put the number in. In this case, we can go over to Error Alert and set the level of the Error along with our own personal message. Now, when I go to put 31000 in, I get this lovely message:

CHARTING – DIFFERENT CHARTS AND THEIR APPLICATIONS

Column Chart

Column charts are pretty flexible in that they will accept nominal data and ordinal data, but the problem is that the more categories you have, the more difficult the graph begins to look at and read. If you have maybe four categories, this type of chart is very easy to read and you can customize it very well. Plus, they can be utilized in other charts so that you can make charts of charts that can further break down the information to a digestible level.

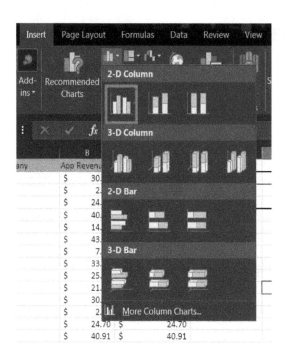

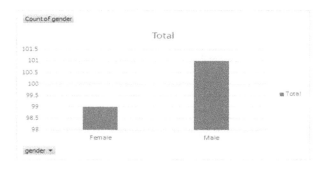

Stacked Column Chart

Stacked column charts are used when you need to measure how much something took part in a whole over periods of time. For example, if you have a research and development department, a marketing department, and a developer department then you would

likely look at all of the salaries in a stacked order to see which

department took up the greatest portion of the budget. If you wanted to

look at this over time, the Stacked column chart would be perfect for

this because then you could look at the same type of data, but you could

look at different segments of time.

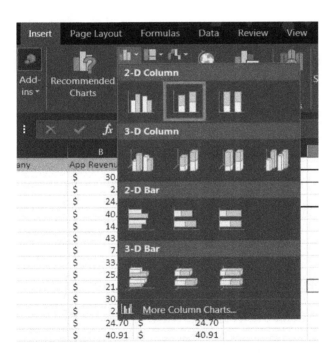

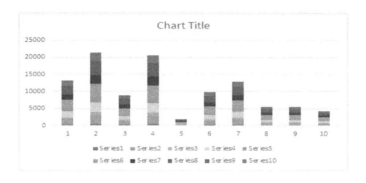

Clustered Column Chart

The clustered column chart is similar to the Stacked column chart but instead of a chart that stacks the blocks on top of each other to represent their portion of the whole, all of the datasets are represented vertically and put together in the time slot you are examining. Therefore, if we went with the Departments that we were looking at before then we would see three departments for quarter one, another three for quarter two, and so on and so forth but each quarter would have different data sets for the three different departments.

Insert	Page Layout	Formulas	Data	Review	View

Add-ins ▾

Recommended Charts

2-D Column

3-D Column

2-D Bar

3-D Bar

📊 More Column Charts...

	B
any	App Revenu
	$ 30.
	$ 2.
	$ 24.
	$ 40.
	$ 14.
	$ 43.
	$ 7.
	$ 33.
	$ 25.
	$ 21.
	$ 30.
	$ 2.
	$ 24.70 $ 24.70
	$ 40.91 $ 40.91

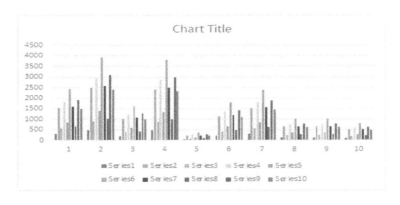

53

Line Chart

This type of chart is as versatile as the column chart and the bar chart but with the ability to handle more categories and more data points than the other two types of charts without confusing the reader too much. On the other hand, the line chart can also confuse things because if there are overlapping multiple lines in different sections then it could look like one solid line or it could look like a messy web. A line chart shows a single line represents a category and then dots or other objects in the line represent different data points such as the dot reaching a price point at a certain time.

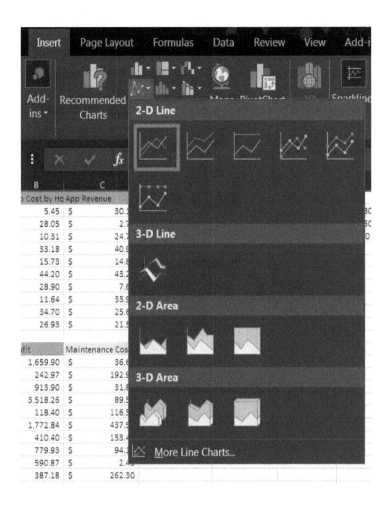

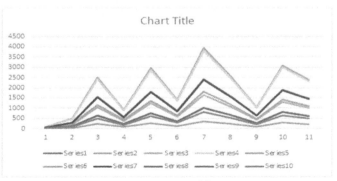

Bar Chart

Bar charts are versatile, and they are easy to apply to almost anything that has several different data points to it, but the problem is that you need categories in order to create bar charts in cells. While it is very easy and versatile to plot data, you can get lost in the number of categories that you have. Additionally, the more data that is added, the more difficult it is to read a bar chart so it's a really good idea to only use bar charts when you only have to account for a few variables. The key distinction of a bar chart is that the data is displayed via a horizontal bar so that you can easily see which variables are more important than others.

Insert	Page Layout	Formulas	Data	Review	View

2-D Column

3-D Column

2-D Bar

3-D Bar

|ılıl| More Column Charts...

	B	
any	App Revenu	
	$	30.
	$	2.
	$	24.
	$	40.
	$	14.
	$	43.
	$	7.
	$	33.
	$	25.
	$	21.
	$	30.
	$	2.
	$	24.70	$	24.70
	$	40.91	$	40.91

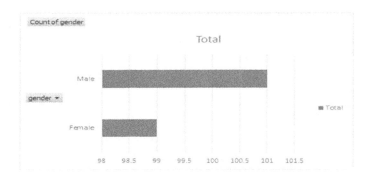

Stacked Bar Chart

As we have already said, bar charts are notably representative by having horizontal bars of data represent the different data points. However, if you want to represent several different sections of a specific category inside of a data point then you want to use a stacked bar chart. A stacked bar chart still utilizes the horizontal lines but is cut up into portions that represent different data sets of a categorical data point. Like the bar chart, it's very simple if you don't have a lot of data and it gets harder to read when there are more data points to go over.

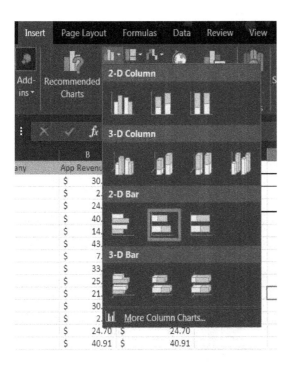

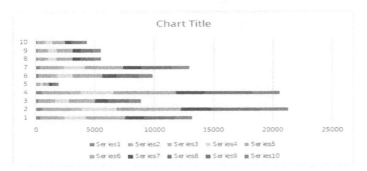

Clustered Bar Chart

The clustered bar chart is similar to the Stacked bar chart but

instead of having the parts take up a whole, the parts are separated in a stack going vertically while the data of those Stacks are represented horizontally. This allows you to further compare the data inside of the data points but as with the Stacked bar chart and the regular bar chart, the more information that there is to handle the more complex and difficult to read it becomes.

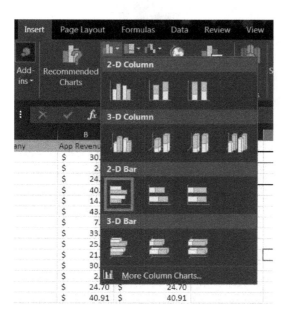

Area Chart

An area chart is a very simplistic way to represent two types of data most of the time, but you can use more than one type of data if you use more than one color. You have your two categories, and these are often a certain amount on the y-axis and then a certain timeline on the

x-axis. The chart will draw a line to all of the data points and at each

data point there will be a non-solid line going downwards towards the

given time. The rest of the graph is then colored in from the line graph

downwards.

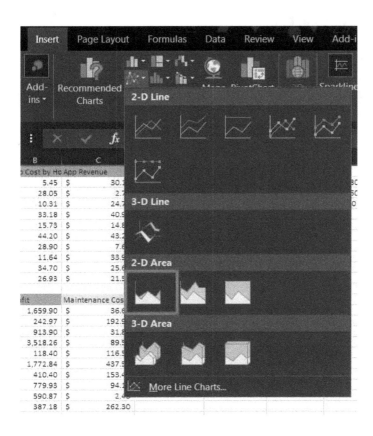

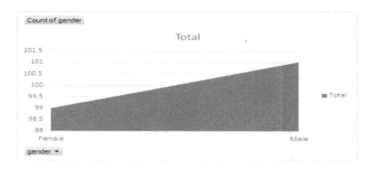

Stacked Area Chart

As I mentioned before, if you use more than one color you can represent more than one type of data set and this is where the Stacked area chart comes in because this is what I was describing. It is a very easy to read graph that is simply for glancing at it and then understanding it without needing to see too much of the information.

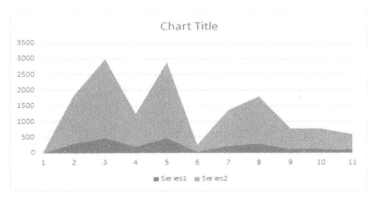

Scatter Plot

Scatter Plots are really good for showing relational data between two or more variables, with the chart usually only representing two variables. The variables themselves are the categories which you used to pinpoint the location of the dot on a scatter plot. Therefore, if you sold 240 t-shirts last year but each t-shirt only sold for $2 then there would be a dot that met at the point where 240 and $2 met in the graph. This would then be represented by repeating this for each of the corresponding data points and then you would be able to look at the scatter plot to where you could draw a line to show a clear representation of what was occurring. Normally, this is often just to show the relational information that one could not easily gain by looking at the numbers. This means that it is really good for scientific data but because of the difficulty of the chart itself, it's not as widely used as something like a bar chart or an area chart. Additionally, if there is no correlation then the graph is basically useless.

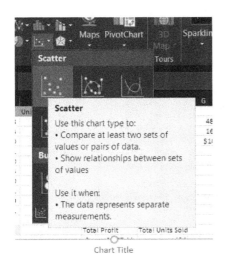

Chart Title

Chart Title

Doughnut Chart

If you have one subject with multiple answers to a question,

then one of the optional charts that you can utilize is a doughnut chart.

Let's say that you're trying to find the favorite fish of everyone in your

state. If you have four different types of fish, then your graph would

look something like this

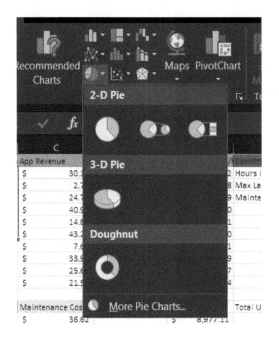

To do this, all you have to have are two columns of data in the

Excel. One side has a name and the other has the quantity, like this:

Bass	4
Grooper	5
Perch	6
Shark	7

This would then allow you go to the Insert Tab -> Click on "Insert Pie or Doughnut" and then choose the doughnut chart from there.

Pie Chart

The pie chart is very easy to implement inside of Excel and it is actually one of the primary charts that you get with the program because it is very easy to represent quantitative data and categorical data with this table chart. Normally, it is represented by categories with numbers that show either a percentage or a specific quantity underneath those categories. This is placed inside of the pie or pointed to at a separate location from the circle that is cut into something that looks like a pie. The problem with this is that the sizes of the pieces are not easily comparable whenever you have a giant quantity of categories and this can also cause a problem with readability if you have more than 8 categories.

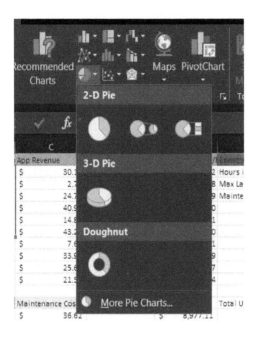

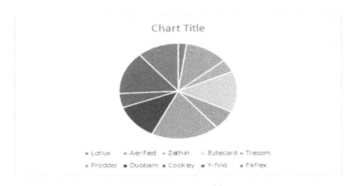

Pie of Pie Chart

Sometimes certain parts of the pie represent more complex data and so a pie of a pie chart is a pie chart that has one piece broken down into a separate pie chart. Again, like the original pie chart, if you have too many categories then it can be very easy to make the data unreadable or lose track of how important certain pie pieces are over others.

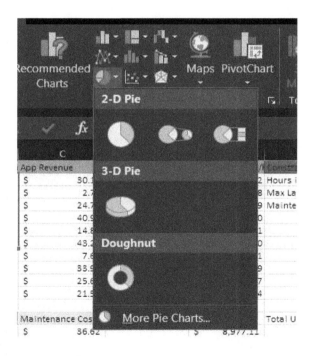

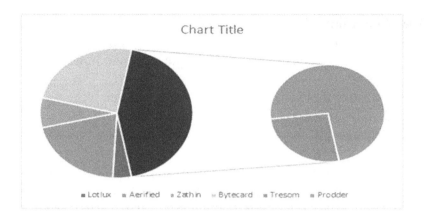

Chart Title

- Lotlux - Aerified - Zathin - Bytecard - Tresom - Prodder

Bar of Pie Chart

Bar of Pie chart is very similar to the pie of pie chart, but it is represented as a stacked bar graph rather than a pie. Needless to say, if you have too many categories in this area then it could be very hard to distinguish or even display that type of data on the screen. However, if you have a certain percentage where you just can't fit all the names in and there were only four or six categories in that specific piece of the pie then you could easily just create a bar of pie chart so that you could represent those off to the side.

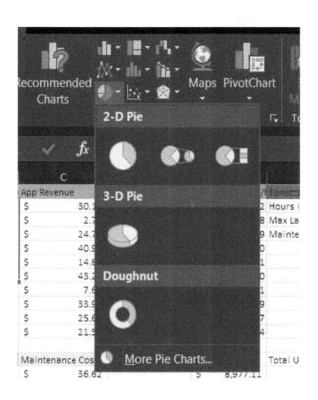

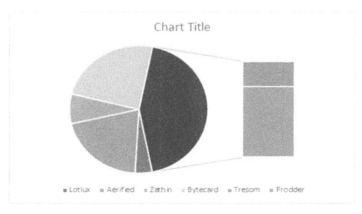

Radar Chart

A radar chart is specifically built to show off key strengths and weaknesses that an individual or a company might have and certain facets of their work areas. You can have as many points as you want but it is very easy to lose the shape of the information by having too many categories resulting in a circular graph where most of the circle goes in a certain direction. So long as you keep the categorical data below 10 aspects then it should be trackable. The idea of this type of chart is that the chart will color the areas where you are strongest while leaving the areas that are your weakest blank. This allows you to look at the graph and easily see it without having to digest too many of the variables to figure out what the graph is telling you.

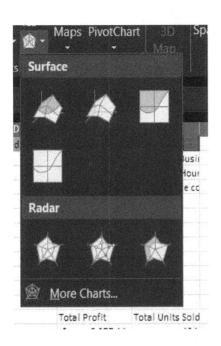

Total Profit | Total Units Sold

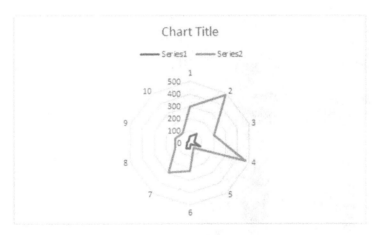

Bubble Chart

Bubble charts are very similar to Scatter Plots because it shows the relationship between variables but what makes a bubble chart unique is that it actually shows clusters of data as Scatter Plots. This means that if you have a certain area where a lot of the data points say the same thing then it will be bigger than other areas in your bubble chart. This is different than a scatter plot because the scatter plot would just put all the dots in the same place and you would just see one dot.

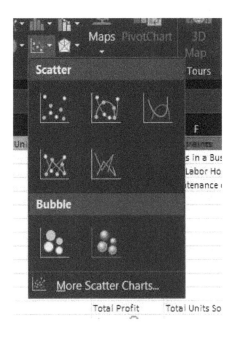

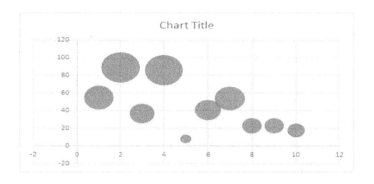

Pareto Chart

The Pareto chart is a very different type of chart and it is somewhat similar to the histogram, but it organizes the data in a descending order. With this type of chart, you are able to have three different categories of data. For instance, if you wanted to compare the revenue increases that you have made through the quarter, but also see a percentage value of it, you could have the exact values on the left-hand side and the percentage values on the right-hand side and then you could have the timeline at the bottom of the screen. This is why the Pareto Chart is quite useful. While one part of the information is represented by bars that go up vertically, another side of the chart is represented by a line that represents the other part of the data in the dataset. Due to its complexity, it can be difficult interpret when first

75

introduced to it, but it does allow you to highlight the sections of data

that are more relevant than others.

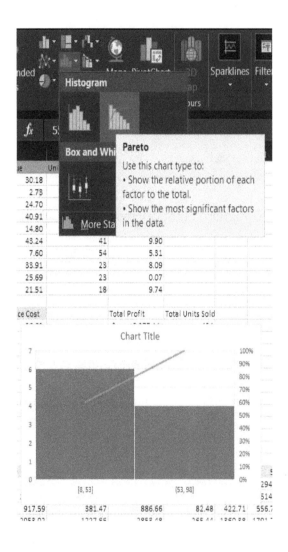

Candlestick Chart

Candlestick charts are actually pretty easy to understand once you tackle the terminology. Candlestick charts are primarily used for stock prices and not much else and you'll see why. Let's say you're looking at a green stick. Obviously, green is good, but what does it mean? Well, on a green stick, the opening price (starting price) for the time period is on the bottom while the closing price (finalized price) is the top of the stick. The green bar represents the growth, but it is called "Real Body". On the red bar, it's the opposite so the opening price is at the top and closing is at the bottom. The vertical line that is not the "Real Body" represents outlier cases on sales where you have the bottom line on both sticks representing lowest price and the top representing the highest price.

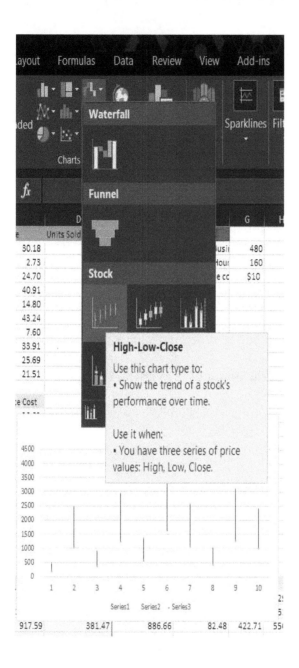

Waterfall Chart

A waterfall chart is fairly easy to understand because it builds on the data from the time period before it. Therefore, if you saw a sales increase of nearly $3,000 in one month and then you not only got that $3,000 but also got $1,200 more the next month, the graph would show that there is a bar that goes vertical showing an increase of $3,000 the first month, the next month would show another bar starting from that location and increasing by $1,200. Additionally, the values are often represented as the increases being on top of the bar and the decreases being below the previous month's bar.

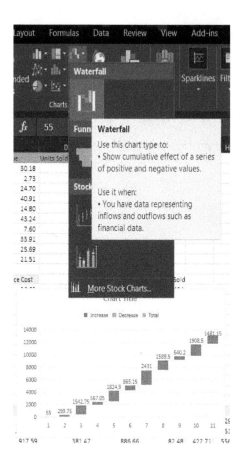

Histogram Chart

A histogram chart is relatively easy to follow because it takes a range of numbers and chops them into groups before it begins to put it in a bar graph. This allows you to represent groups of numbers at a time and so it makes a graph much easier to read. It basically gives you a frequency of each number or relevant categories. It's very easy to make and it provides a very easy way to read it without having to go deeper into the variables but since it's not very common, most people would mistake it for a bar chart so it may not be the easiest to read if you are introducing this to a crowd of individuals not used to seeing histogram charts.

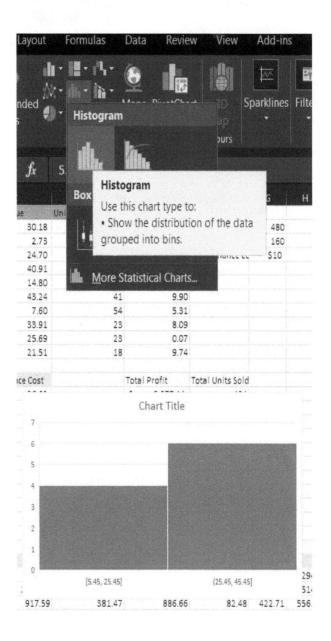

Treemap Chart

A treemap chart is a confusing mess if you don't know how to read it and so it is almost exclusively used by those who program a lot. It allows you to do several different things depending on what you're trying to accomplish. For instance, you can have several different categories with other categories inside of it. The datasets inside of those original categories are often represented proportionally by rectangles or squares that show how much of a portion that that data set is taking up of the overall category.

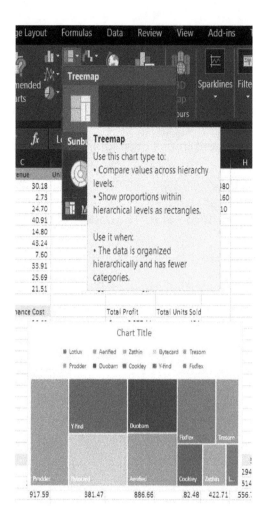

Sunburst Chart

The Sunburst chart is a lot like the doughnut chart but it actually

shows a hierarchical chain of data inside of the graph going from the

inside to the outside of the graph:

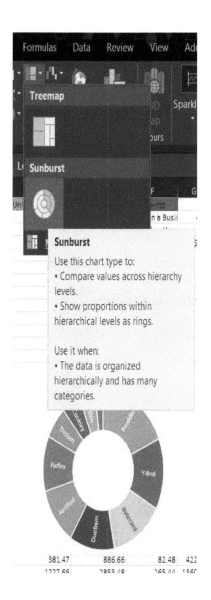

Combo Chart

A combo chart is really just a combination of two different charts put together so that you can represent more data points inside of a graph than you would normally be able to with a specific type of data. For instance, if you wanted to represent the years in which revenues took place and then also point out production values at that time then you could show a bar graph that represents the revenues while a line graph represented the production values at that time.

USING CORRELATIONS TO SUMMARIZE APPLICATIONS

What is Correlation Analysis?

Correlation analysis is often easy to understand but difficult to implement and this is due to the way in which you might implement it. Correlation analysis is really the study of seeing how similar things are to themselves. For instance, if you were to compare Capital One to Credit One, you could say that they were similar in the fact that they were both a type of credit card company, but you might also say they were not similar in how they went about handling their customer service procedure. The important thing to realize with correlation analysis is that the analysis is done by comparing each point with another point. In Excel, we utilize columns and rows, so if your comparative data is inside of a column then your data that you are comparing it to will also need to be in a column and vice versa. Additionally, the number that you get back is either a -1, a 0, or a 1. A 1 represents that the correlation is very similar while a -1 represents a correlation that is not similar.

Why is it useful?

Correlation analysis is very useful because it allows you to compare two things on a massive scale and to conceptualize whether the overall impact that you have is significant or not. For instance, if you are trying to see if the increase in your profit is because of a rise in customer service satisfaction then you'd be able to take the responses that you got from the surveys that the customers completed after they were done with their customer service call and compare that to the times in which profit was high. If there was a correlation, then you would see the program output any number between 0.7 and 1. For a negative correlation, you would see an output between -0.7 and -1. Anything outside those values shows that the data is uncorrelated.

Note: Just because two sets of data are correlated does not mean that one causes the other. For example, in the summer in Chicago; you will see a correlation between the number of murders and ice cream sales.

This is because both happen during the summer. It does not mean that ice cream sales cause an increase in murders.

How to Do it in Excel?

It is very easy to do this inside of Excel, which is hard to say for some programs out there that are built to handle statistics, but this could be because of how the different systems judge the data such as the Pearson system that works from digits from 0 to 1 rather than -1 to 1 and similar judging parameters. First, you have 2 rows or columns that have numerical comparative data in them. Then you make sure that Data Analysis is available to you by going into Options > Add-ins to turn on the Analysis ToolPak, which is used for further Data Analysis. Be sure to choose the non-VBA one because the VBA one is for programmers. Now you will be able to find Data Analysis in the Analyze tab where you found Solver. Clicking on it will bring up a list of different tools. Select Correlation, then click OK. This will then bring up this dialogue box:

First, you have the input range, which is your comparative data. Then you have whether that data is in columns or rows. Finally, you have the area you want to display it. Once you click ok, it will do several different correlations. It will check if Column 1 is similar to Column 2, then it will check if Column 2 is similar to Column 2, then it will check if Column 1 is similar to Column 1, and then it will check if Column 2 is similar to Column 1. It does this because the correlation might change depending on the way you may be comparing the data, but this is how you perform a correlation analysis in Excel.

DATA FILTERS

Data filters are a great way to be able to sort through different items inside of a given dataset. So, if you have anything over 50 different items, it is extremely useful to be able to filter through those items. A perfect example of this is a bank account and so I have generated a randomized bank account that allows us to see the benefits of this filtering.

Singular Filters

The first type of filter that we are going to go through is the singular filter and that allows you to choose on a specific header in your data set so that you can select a way of filtering it. For instance, let's say that I only wanted to look at the accounts that were owned by male individuals. The first thing that I would do is I would go up to the filter option in the editing section.

This will then bring over some drop down arrows that I can

click on and it will bring me to a different type of menu.

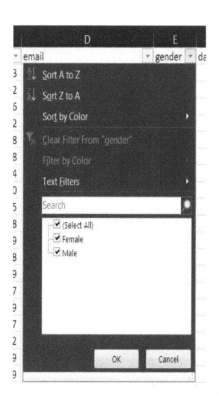

As you can see, I can unselect the checkbox that says female and

it will remove all the female rows that are in this list. Keep in mind that

it doesn't just remove the females from the gender column but the entire row that has female in it in the gender column. This will not delete the data, but filter it to just show all the rows that are labeled male in the gender category. In order to go and get it back, all you have to do is re-click the filter button to turn off the filter.

Multi-Filters

It is actually fairly easy to do multiple filters because if you have more than one available option Excel will detect the common multiples and you just click on the ones you don't want. What this will do is it will only display the values that are currently selected. Likewise, if you have all of the items colored differently such as invoices are green if you are charging a customer and invoices are red or orange if you are being charged, you can select the sort by color in the same drop down.

The Advanced Options

The advanced options for filtering are still within this same menu. If you look back at the drop-down menu you will see something called text filters and inside of text filters you have several different options you can utilize. Normally, you can compare strings so that you can get ones that equal a word you're searching for or you can get ones that don't equal the word that you are trying to exclude. Likewise, you have the option of finding bits of text that begin with certain characters or contain certain characters. Finally, you do have the option of detecting whether a certain word is contained within all of the text or if it is not contained within all of the text and you have the option of developing your own custom filter. Each type of data will have its own type of advanced filter such as a number filter or a date filter. The important thing to realize is that it really depends on what type of data is actually inside of the cell you are working with. For instance, if you are dealing with binary values like male or female, you don't really have a need to go that complex into searching them but if you were to look through a ton of emails then you would likely want the text filter to be able to look for all the emails that happened to be from Yahoo or from Gmail. Excel will automatically detect what type of item is inside each cell and will give you an automatically-generated advanced filter based off what it detects. Therefore, if there is a collection of letters then it will assume that it is a form of text, but if the data is formatted as 01-01-2017 or 01-JAN-2017 it will automatically detect that this is the format used in dates.

DATA CONSOLIDATION

What is Data Consolidation?

Data consolidation is when you take the data that you are working with and you remove the unnecessary multiples of that data. For instance, say that Sally has made 14 purchases and John has made 34. Well, in a banking transaction you would see 14 separate purchases and 34 separate purchases. However, if you just wanted to know how much money you made from Sally or John, you would want to consolidate the data so that it only takes up two spots and that all that information has been added up for your convenience so that you can easily see who gave you more money and how much money you made overall.

Why should you do it?

While I did just use a very basic example, that isn't the only way that data consolidation can be used. If you've done a survey and are trying to calculate the responses of everyone from a sample size of nearly a thousand people, it would be a nightmare to go through each and every individual and count their response. Instead, you can consolidate based on what is in that column and calculate the percentages of the responses that you've gotten from your sample size.

If you are trying to find out how much revenue you made and how much money you can give your research and development department, you can easily go through all of the purchases that the research and development department made and then head over to a second spreadsheet that might contain your relative information about how much you made on the market and then you can use data consolidation to easily find how much money you made versus how much money was spent. This is applicable to any situation where you have more than one label for the same type of data and you are wanting to combine that data.

How to do it in Excel?

In the Data tab, you will find the "Consolidate" button, which will look like this:

By clicking on it, you come to this menu:

The function is the way you want to Consolidate your information and this list is not exhaustive. The reference is the area that you want to consolidate, and this includes the labels/names. You will always be collecting at least 2 columns when you use this button. Once you select the area, you also have the ability to select others in other worksheets with the All References as you will see when you look at how Consolidate highlights it:

Now, it is important in this case to let Excel know that we are using labels from the left row so we hit that checkmark. Then we click Ok. Now it will automatically generate a consolidated list in the right-hand corner, like this:

Lotlux	$	90.54
Aerified	$	8.19
Zathin	$	74.10
Bytecard	$	122.73
Tresom	$	44.40
Prodder	$	129.72
Duobam	$	22.80
Cookley	$	101.73
Y-find	$	77.07
Fixflex	$	64.53

To select data from other worksheets, you just need to type in the sheet and then the cell range you want to work with.

OTHER FUNCTIONS

SUMIFS

The SUMIFS formula is absolutely amazing because it allows you to use more than one condition. Previously, if you used the SUMIF formula, you would have had to use several in order to do complex conditional formulas. The SUMIFS allows you to reduce all of those SUMIF formulas into a singular formula. In order to use a SUMIFS, you need to have more than one condition. When dealing with any IFS functions, because there's way more than just SUMIFS, it is very important to understand the three key terms discussed next. Additionally, if you have not learned any of the IF functions that can be IFS, just learn the IFS as they are generally better. The three key terms are:

Criteria Range

Okay, so Criteria Range is actually very simple and confusing to understand. The part that is simple is that the Criteria Range represents the column of data you are looking through to find values in your X Range. Therefore, if you are looking for a specific country among a long list of countries then the list of countries is your Criteria Range while the specific country you are looking for is your Criteria. The part that is confusing is that your Criteria Range can also be your X Range in some cases. For instance, let's say you are using SUMIFS so that your X Range becomes SUM_RANGE. If you are trying to find a value that is greater than 200 amongst a range of numbers and the SUM_RANGE is going to be the range of numbers, the Criteria Range is *also* going to be a range of numbers. Then your Criteria is going to be the condition of >200.

Criteria

Criteria means Condition in this case. This can be numerical or not, so it can be categorized by saying that you want to filter through X department or it can be numerical, and you can say that you only want numbers >200.

X Range

I put this as X Range because almost all of the IFS will have their own range variables such as the SUMIFS having a sum_range and the COUNTIFS having a count_range. This is the range that you are going to apply the Criteria Range and Criteria to.

Now that you understand these three terms, you can fully read the

SUMIFS(sum_range, criteria_range1, criteria1, [criteria_range2, criteria2], ...)

What this is saying is that you must first select the numbers you are summing together. Then you need to select the range that your criteria/condition will affect (the Criteria Range). If you decide you want more, you just repeat the actions of adding another criteria range and then another criterion. This is how the SUMIFS formula works and it is massively more powerful than the SUMIF formula.

SUMPRODUCT

Mathematically, this is actually pretty easy to understand but a little difficult to apply, which is why it is one of the advanced formulas. An array is a collection of things, for example counting one to ten would be an array of one to ten. The SUMPRODUCT takes in up to 255 different arrays. Then it multiplies those arrays but in sequential order so say we have 3-digit arrays and we have 2 of them. The first digit from the first array would be multiplied by the first digit from the second array and so on and so forth. Once it had multiplied each of them by the corresponding digit (1st with 1st, 2nd with 2nd) it will then add all of those together.

VLOOKUP

This formula is pretty easy to understand but it does require the same type of knowledge that you just gained from learning how the different IF statements work. First, you need a spot where the formula is going to display the output and this can be a singular cell or can be multiple cells. This will be where you put the formula. For our example, we will search for an employee number in a table. The first argument in the formula will then be the output cell where the formula will place the output. Then you need the area in which the formula is going to search for both the identifying marker and the criteria marker. The identifying marker is the information that you know such as the name Becky, what you don't know is the criteria marker which is the employee number that is attached to Becky. Then you have the third argument, which can be quite confusing if you're not familiar with it. Imagine that the area that you told the formula to look in is a separate spreadsheet and each column is represented by a number going from 1 to infinity. Therefore, if your area is made up of 3 columns and the information that you want to find is in the second column of those 3 columns, then your third parameter would be the numerical value of 2. Finally, you have to tell the formula if you want to search for an exact match or if you just care about whether it is generally a good match. You provide false if you want an exact match and true if you want a general match. The final formula should look something like this:

=VLOOKUP(F3,B3:D1000,2,FALSE)

What this is saying is that we want the cell F3 to be where the input is, we want the search area to go from B3 to D1000. Finally, of the columns B, C, and D, we want column 2, otherwise known as C, to be the search area for the criteria marker and we want an exact match. When you first place this in, the output result will actually be a not applicable result. It is only when you put an input in the F3 spot that you will receive some appropriate form of output.

INDEX MATCH

INDEX MATCH was there before VLOOKUP and many advanced users prefer to use INDEX MATCH over VLOOKUP because it is not as limited as VLOOKUP since VLOOKUP can only look through column data whereas INDEX MATCH can be applied to rows and columns to do almost the same thing. The only difference is that you are looking up what is inside of an index rather than the relatable data that we used in VLOOKUP. I believe you might begin to see why both methods are here at this point. In order to use INDEX MATCH, you must first hand it a range to look through and then the index number you want to look at. Therefore you could have C1:Z1 and provide it with 5 and it would give you the value that was in H1 or if

you have C1:C100 and you gave it 50, it would give you the value in

C:50. Something to keep in mind is that it sees the first cell as index 1,

so we could tell it to look through C50:C100 for index 25 and it would

return C:75 since C:50 would be index 1.

Handling Formula Errors and Formula Auditing

When we talk about handling formula errors you might be

thinking that this involves you figuring out how to change your formula

if it provides you an error, but the honest truth is that this is not how

you handle errors given to you by formulas. If you are given an error

and you need to be able to compensate for that error because most of

the equation is right, then you use something called the IFERROR

formula. What this formula does is provide you a way of catching an

error as it happens and providing a default value if that error occurs. For

instance, if you have calculations that assume that you will be making a

profit most of the time, then when you don't make a profit then it's

going to provide you with an error. In order to handle this, you would

use this type of formula. It is very simple to use this formula because all you need for the first argument is the expected value or condition that can occur to provide your error, and then the second argument is just the value that you should give if that error occurs.

However, error-handling is not just about using a singular formula because you will have several different errors that happen simply because you may have missed a letter, or your column isn't wide enough to fit the value inside of it. If your column isn't wide enough to fit a value inside of it, you will get a series of pound signs inside of the cell that's being affected. On the other hand, if there is an actual identification of what type of problem that the cell is having then you can click on the Error Help Icon.

Clicking on this button will help you search through all the known errors that are occurring inside of your application, and this will be different depending on the error. However, that isn't always going to help you and this is the point of formula auditing. If you are getting an error inside of your formula then the error can be subject to the formula auditing tab, which is where you find the error helper. For instance, if you get the value error and it is because you have manually added or multiplied all the specific cells that you want without using the automatic formulas like you should have been using, you can use the trace precedents or trace dependents to show the path that the formula is taking in order to complete the equation.

CONCLUSION

Understanding Why Being Advanced in Excel is Important

A lot of people dislike Excel because of how clunky it can feel at first and truth be told I can't argue against this because it is a very intimidating program if you are just opening it up for the first time. The problem then becomes that you need to explain why being an advanced user in Excel is actually a very beneficial thing and the problem with this is it is very similar to asking a math teacher where you are going to apply a certain type of math. The math teacher can't give you a quantitative answer because there are so many applications to that mathematical application. Trying to answer your question is mind-blowingly difficult. I think the best way that I can put this is an experience that I had with a friend of mine. This woman was a bookkeeper that had been a proponent of QuickBooks for a number of years and she believed that there was nothing that QuickBooks could do that Excel could also do. This is because Excel is seen often as a spreadsheet program and nothing more than a spreadsheet program.

However, you can make Excel do everything that QuickBooks does and you can have more control over how it does it than the proprietary software of QuickBooks. One of the items that this woman suggested to me was that you could not make a checking register inside of Excel and this was ridiculous, but I had to explain how Excel could do this. After showing her that Excel could do this, she then proceeded to ask why I want to program in all the features of QuickBooks when I have QuickBooks available and this is a valid point. However, if you are at the start of your business and you are able to create your own checking system and your own balancing system, you will have full control over all the variables and aspects of your business without relying on black boxes. QuickBooks doesn't give you that much control and, to the pros and cons of many, QuickBooks also refuses the ability to acknowledge that you have deleted something from the system. Instead, most of the time the change is acknowledged, the item is removed, but it is represented by a red out area or some fashion that shows you that the item still exists, but it was just removed by another user. In other words, if you make a lot of mistakes inside of QuickBooks because your organization is still trying to organize themselves and get all their factors right, QuickBooks can be devastating because of all the different errors that can happen. Additionally, that just includes whether there was a mistake that you did because there are tons of mistakes that can happen in the financial area of QuickBooks that are caused by someone other than the bookkeeper. Every time that you make a change in this program, you will then have to make changes in other parts of the program so that QuickBooks is back to a working condition that you can use. Excel doesn't have this pesky feature and so while it may not be ideal for filing taxes, it makes it exceedingly easy to not only keep track of what you need to keep track of but to also to change something without needing to make system-wide changes. Additionally, if you wanted the functionality that QuickBooks has that keeps track of items that are changed then you can use the advanced features of Excel to ensure that this happens. You can recreate QuickBooks inside of Excel but also have all of the benefits

that come with working inside of Excel.

How This Skill Translates

Excel is used by business individuals, people who work in the

data science industry, technicians who are trying to crunch numbers that

are massive, basic accounting individuals, people who run their entire

bookkeeping department off Excel sheets alone. The list really does go

on for the number of people that use Excel in their industry, but it

doesn't get a lot of credit. Excel is seen as one of those secondary

programs that people only utilize whenever it is convenient or whenever

they don't have access to their main program. The professionals that

work in the data science industry and the industries that see Excel as a

gift from the programming heavens are not able to communicate to the

more basic users why Excel is so powerful and how it can actually

change a lot of the ways that you work in your environment. If you are

doing anything with numbers, anything means any industry that is

based on numbers such as data science, finance, sometimes legal,

bookkeeping, indexing, database management, etc., Excel is like having the ability to program without learning how to program. You can make Excel do pretty much anything you want with numbers and the number of built-in features that Excel has is mind-bogglingly huge. This is why being an advanced user of Excel translates to almost every industry.

It's Pure Fun

Honestly, I have to say that it was pure fun just digging out new toys from this huge toy box that looks so small. You are not the only one to think that this was just a spreadsheet program and that it didn't have much functionality to it. You are not the only one who thought that this program could give you some usefulness, but it couldn't be so massive. If you didn't think these then no harm no foul, but most people will see Excel as a very simplistic and basic program until they start digging out the toys from the toy box. This program is so bleak looking that it comes off as not being as powerful as it really is and so whenever you begin to open it up, it turns into this massive power-hungry software that can almost to do everything except that no one decided to give it anything outside of numbers. Learning all the advanced features that Excel has for you is like getting a new toy. That is why I have been referring to it as this because when you learn that you can do a certain type of thing inside of Excel that you thought wasn't possible, it becomes your new toy and you want to try and use it on something. It's honestly fun at this point to find new things inside of a program you thought you mostly knew.

A Final Word

I have refrained from saying that Excel can do everything, and that Excel has nothing but benefits. The truth of the matter is that this is a software and every software always has a downside. Software isn't supposed to be able to do everything, at least not yet, and so while Excel can do a ton of different things, that doesn't mean that it should. I did mention earlier that people who know the programming language can actually automate their entire job but knowing how much power goes behind that is kind of scary. For instance, telling people that their paychecks are going to be run by an automated system may mean that those people are either going to take advantage of the system, because you might have forgotten to set up an alert that will tell you if anybody is working an abnormal number of hours, or that system just accidentally does not pay anyone for a week because something went wrong with the automation. When you automate something, you take it out of your hands and put it into the flawed hands of your creation. You cannot say that you will ever make the perfect program and so your program is bound to have a glitch or two that you didn't account for. It is important to always have a human hand guiding the program because the program can't think for itself and can't notice when it's doing something wrong. As powerful as Excel may be, that also means that you have to keep an eye on how much you use Excel in your industry because it could easily mess you up. Having said that, Excel should not be something you should be afraid of and it is definitely a very useful tool that everyone should at least try their hands at. This powerful software can do so much more than the average user knows and this is probably why bookkeeping positions are seeking Excel experts more than they are seeking anyone else. The fact of the matter is that Excel has become a very powerful program that can compete with the best programs out there that deal with numbers and so this book was to help introduce you to some of the more advanced aspects of Excel. I hope you truly enjoyed this book and I look forward to helping you next time.

www.ingramcontent.com/pod-product-compliance
Lightning Source LLC
Chambersburg PA
CBHW071550080326
40690CB00056B/1621